1. INTRODUCTION

Over two decades since its emergence, payday lending remains a divisive topic for economists and policymakers. No conscensus has been reached on whether access to these high-cost, short-term balloon loans makes consumers better off or worse. Advocates point to cases where payday loans appear to be a customer's best option. For instance, if unexpected medical expenses leave a family short on money to pay utilities, a payday loan may be preferable to an electricity shutoff and eventual reconnect fee. Alternative sources of funds may be unavailable in the case of emergency (for instance, credit cards may be maxed out) or more expensive than payday loans (as are overdraft fees at many banks). Research such as Morgan and Strain (2008), Elliehausen (2009), Fusaro and Cirillo (2011), and Morse (2011) has supported the notion that access to payday lending is welfare-enhancing.

However, opponents of payday lending point out that customers rarely report borrowing in response to such emergency situations. Pew Charitable Trusts (2012) finds that only 16% of payday customers took out their initial loan in response to an unexpected expense, while 69% reported borrowing to cover a recurring expense such as rent or groceries. In addition, though they are marketed as short-term loans designed to deal with transitory shocks, a significant fraction of customers use payday loans repeatedly.[1] Such repeat borrowing fuels the claim that payday loans can trap borrowers in cycles of debt. Research such as Parrish and King (2009), Melzer (2011), and Carrell and Zinman (2013) suggests that the damage caused by such debt cycles outweighs the benefits of access.

Given the continued debate over its merits and the long history of high-cost, short-term loans aimed at credit-compromised customers (Caskey, 1996) it seems likely that payday lending, or something similar to it, will remain a feature of the credit landscape for the forseeable future. For

---

[1] The exact fraction of payday lending that should be considered repeat borrowing is a contentious subject. The distribution of borrowing is heavily skewed, with occasional borrowers making up the bulk of the customers but repeat borrowers making up the bulk of the loans. This causes statistics to vary drastically according to whether they are person-weighted or loan-weighted, and whether the mean or median is considered. In addition, statistics vary according to whether repeat borrowing is defined as an unbroken string of loans or as the number of loans within a fixed time period. Rather than report simple summary statistics, Table 1 presents a range of percentiles in order to more comprehensively characterize the distribution of borrowing.

this reason it may be productive to ask not whether payday lending is good or bad on net, but instead which *type* of payday lending would be best.

Both sides of the debate tend to treat "payday lending" as a monolithic entity, but in practice it is a pastiche of practices shaped by a diverse set of state laws. States have approached payday lending with a variety of regulatory strategies including price caps, size caps, prohibitions on repeat borrowing, prohibitions on simultaneous borrowing, "cooling-off" periods, mandates to provide amortizing alternatives, and many combinations thereof. Some of these forms of regulation may create payday loans that lead to better outcomes than others. Though a few papers, notably Avery and Samolyk (2011), have attempted to compare regulations of differing strengths (in the case of Avery and Samolyk (2011), higher price caps versus lower ones), efforts to distinguish among regulatory strategies have so far been limited.

This paper breaks down the monolith of payday lending in order to judge the relative merits of lending under different regulatory regimes. It uses a novel institutional dataset covering all loans originated by a single large payday lender between January 2007 and August 2012, in 26 of the 36 states in which payday lending is allowed—a total of over 56 million loans. Unlike previous payday datasets, the depth and breadth of these data span a variety of regulatory environments, making it possible to estimate of the effects of a variety of regulatory approaches.

However, the data are also limited in some ways. Most importantly, customer activity outside of payday borrowing is unobserved, making it impossible to estimate effects on overall financial health. Second, because the data come from a single lender one cannot credibly estimate the effect of state laws on total lending volume. For these reasons this paper focuses on loan terms and usage-based outcomes. In particular, it focuses on customers' propensity to borrow repeatedly. Whatever their other views, payday lending's supporters and detractors often tend to agree that very persistent indebtedness is undersirable and indicative of counterproductive use, making repeat borrowing a useful object of study.

I find that payday loan price caps tend to be strictly binding on prices, while size caps are much less binding on loan size. Prohibitions on simultaneous borrowing appear to have little effect on total amount borrowed. Minimum term limits affect loan length, but maximum term limits do not. Sources of delinquency are difficult to identify, though delinquency seems positively related to higher price caps. Repeat borrowing appears negatively related to rollover prohibitions and cooling-off periods, as well as to higher price caps. Extended repayment options have little identifiable effect, though that may be due in part to idiosyncracies of the dataset. Looking at individual states that changed their laws, South Carolina, Virginia, and Washington all enacted changes that significantly cut their rates of repeat borrowing. These changes were accompanied by significant upheavals, particularly in Virginia and Washington where loan volume plummeted and, in the case of Virginia, delinquency spiked.

Section 2 provides background on the payday lending industry and the state regulations that affect it. Section 3 describes the data, the sources of regulatory variation, and the econometric specifications. Section 4 presents results using cross-state pooled regressions and within-state law-change regressions. Section 5 concludes.

2. PAYDAY LENDING AND STATE REGULATION

Payday lending is widespread. FDIC (2013) estimates that 4.7% of all U.S. households have at some time used payday lending, while Pew Charitable Trusts (2012) puts the figure at 5.5% of U.S. adults. In 2005, payday storefronts outnumbered McDonald's and Starbucks locations combined (Graves and Peterson, 2008). Lenders extended $40 billion in payday credit in 2010, generating revenues of $7.4 billion (Stephens Inc., 2011).

To date the federal government has not directly regulated payday lending (save via general statutes such as the Truth in Lending Act and the Military Lending Act), though this may change now that the Consumer Financial Protection Bureau (CFPB) has been given rulemaking authority over the industry. Traditionally, payday lending regulation has been left to the states. Prior to the mid-2000s, states' ability to regulate payday lending was undermined by the so-called "rent-a-bank" model, wherein a local lender would partner with a federally-chartered bank not subject to that lender's state laws, thereby importing exemption from those laws (Mann and Hawkins, 2007; Stegman, 2007). In March 2005 the Federal Deposit Insurance Corporation (FDIC) issued guidance effectively prohibiting banks from using this model, giving state laws more bite.

The advent of online payday lending offers a potential alternative model for skirting state law. However, initial evidence suggests only very limited substitution between storefront and online payday products. Online payday customers tend to be younger, richer, and more educated than storefront customers, and states that ban storefront payday have virtually identical rates of online borrowing as states that allow storefront payday (Pew Charitable Trusts, 2012). This suggests that customers have not responded to more stringent state regulations by substituting toward online payday in appreciable numbers.

2.1. **The payday lending model.** A payday loan is structured as a short-term advance on a paycheck. The borrower provides proof of employment (usually via pay stubs) and writes a check for the principal of the loan plus the fee, post-dated for after the next payday. For instance, a borrower might write a check for $345 and walk out with $300 in cash. Once the payday arrives the lender cashes the check written by the borrower.

Though payday loans are technically uncollateralized, the lender's possession of the post-dated check (or, increasingly often, the permission to directly debit the borrower's checking account) plays a collateral-like role. By taking the repayment decision out of the borrower's hands, payday lenders effectively ensure they are repaid ahead of the borrower's other debts and expenses. Though default is still possible, loss rates of around 3.5% of loan volume (Stephens Inc., 2011) are very low given borrower creditworthiness.[2] The high price of payday loans reflects their high overhead cost more than it does high losses from default. Stephens Inc. (2011) estimates that in 2010 losses comprised only 21% of total cost.[3]

Because payday loans are typically due on the borrower's next payday, terms of 14 days are common. Given prices around $15 per $100 borrowed, APRs are often in the range of 300%–500%.

---

[2]Bhutta, Skiba, and Tobacman (2012) finds that payday applicants have an average Equifax credit score of 513.
[3]Flannery and Samolyk (2007) argues that the payday industry's high overhead is due to low barriers to entry. Each loan is profitable but demand is relatively fixed and price-insensitive, so storefronts enter the market and compete over scarce lending opportunities until each one just covers its overhead. This story is consistent with the large number of stores in operation, and with each store's relatively low lending volume (an average of 15.3 loans per store per day in my data). If these arguments are correct they imply that stricter price caps will reduce the number of storefronts, causing each store to operate at more efficient scale, without actually inhibiting lending. Avery and Samolyk (2011) offers evidence in support of this conclusion. In my data there is a correlation of -0.54 between price caps and loan volume per store. Likewise, regression estimates imply that dropping the cap by $10 per $300 borrowed raises loans per store by 10.9%, equivalent to 1.7 loans per day.

On the due date the whole amount of the loan is due in a single balloon payment. Borrowers wishing to renew their loan can theoretically recreate the structure of an amortizing loan by borrowing slightly less each time. In practice, it is much more common for customers to borrow the same amount with each renewal until such time as the loan can be retired.

2.2. **Strategies to regulate payday lending.** States concerned about payday lending within their borders have passed a variety of laws to regulate it. The following list details the most widely-used regulatory strategies.

2.2.1. *Price caps.* A very common form of payday lending regulation is price caps. States that "prohibit" payday lending usually do so by setting APR caps that are too low for the payday business model to profitably operate, effectively driving lenders from the state. Caps of 36% APR are used by many states for this purpose. States with caps high enough to allow payday lending also may use APR limits, but more commonly the caps are stated as a dollar limit per amount lent. A cap of $15 per $100 is typical. Some states use tiered schedules of price caps: for instance, Indiana limits fees to 15% of the first $250 lent, 13% of the next $251-$400, and 10% of anything above that.

2.2.2. *Size caps.* Many states limit the maximum size of a payday loan. The modal size limit is $500. Some states don't use a fixed size limit but instead set the limit as a percentage of the borrower's monthly income. Size limits are meant to limit a borrower's ability to become indebted, though they can potentially be circumvented in states that allow borrowers to take multiple loans at a time.

2.2.3. *Loan term limits.* Maximum term limits put an upper cap on the length of a payday loan. Minimum term limits potentially directly address one of the alleged problems with payday loans: short maturity that leaves borrowers scrambling to repay by the due date. By requiring longer minimum terms, states might give customers the time necessary to sort out their finances before the loan is due. However, if the main source of repayment difficulty is that the loan doesn't amortize, a slightly longer balloon loan may be no easier to retire than a slightly shorter one. Some states don't use a fixed minimum loan term, but instead vary the minimum according to the length of the borrower's pay period.

2.2.4. *Limits on simultaneous borrowing.* Some states set limits on the absolute number of loans a customer can borrow at a given time, while others set limits on the number of loans a customer can borrow from a single lender at a given time. The former type of regulation requires that there be some way for the lender to check the activity of other lenders; the latter type does not. For this reason, limits on the absolute number of simultaneous loans are often enacted along with legislation establishing a statewide loan database.

2.2.5. *Rollover prohibitions.* Prohibitions on renewing ("rolling over") loans are extremely popular, though their efficacy is debated. Superficially, rollover bans seem like a good tool to address the problem of repeat borrowing. In practice, these laws may at times be circumvented by paying off the first loan and then immediately taking out a second loan, which is technically not the same loan as the first. States vary according to how a rollover is defined and in the number of rollovers, if any, that they permit. Some states permit rollovers only if a portion of the principal is paid down.

2.2.6. *Cooling-off periods.* After a period of repeat borrowing some states require a "cooling-off" period, which is a length of time during which borrowing is not allowed. Cooling-off periods vary in length, though 1 to 10 days is common, and may be triggered according to the number of consecutive loans or by the total number of loans in the year. Like rollover prohibitions, cooling-off periods are an attempt to directly prohibit repeat borrowing.

2.2.7. *Extended repayment options.* A number of states require that under certain circumstances lenders make available an extended, amortizing loan option in addition to their basic payday loan option. Extended repayment loans may be made available after a certain number of rollovers, or may be always available. There is a huge degree of variation among states in the form that the extended repayment options take. Most states only require that the option be made available; they do not require that the option be used.[4] Variation between states in extended repayment options

---

[4]Colorado has enacted a unique law that entirely replaces payday loans with an extended repayment option. Unfortunately, Colorado is not included in this dataset.

may be somewhat muted in this dataset because the lender that provided the data, unlike many lenders, makes extended repayment options available even in states where they are not required.

3. THE DATA

The data in this paper were provided by a large, anonymous payday lender and consist of all loans made by this lender in 26 states between January 2007 and August 2012. Figure 1 maps the states included in the data. The data contain no demographic information about borrowers, but loans made to the same borrower can be linked across time and location. The street address of the storefront at which the loan was made is known. The data include all dimensions of the loan contract, as well as its repayment history. The lender makes no direct online loans, though it refers customers to online lending affiliates through its website. The dataset contains only directly made storefront loans.

The data consist of 56,143,566 loans made at 2,906 different stores to 3,428,271 distinct customers. Once simultaneous loans are combined and considered as single loans (as explained below) this number drops to 54,119,468, for an average of 15.8 loans per customer. However, the median number of loans per customer is 7, reflecting the skewness of the distribution. Table 1 presents distributions for many variables in the data.

3.1. **Variable Definitions.** Because payday loans vary in size, price, and length of term, any comparisons should be robust to relabeling. For instance, two simultaneous loans of $250 should be considered equivalent to a single loan of $500—it would be problematic to conclude that in the former case "twice as much" payday lending had occurred as in the latter, since all that must be done to convert one scenario to the other is relabel. Similarly, a customer who takes out twelve 1-week loans in a row, paying $20 each time, and a customer who takes out two 6-week loans at a cost of $120 each, should be treated similarly. Though superficially the former had 11 rollovers while the latter had only one, in each case the customer spent exactly 12 consecutive weeks in debt and paid $240.

In order to construct outcome variables that are agnostic to labeling I depart slightly from standard practice. Rather than count sequences of consecutive loans, my main repeat borrowing measure is a binary variable measuring whether, exactly 90 days after origination of the current loan, the customer again has an active loan.[5] This definition is agnostic about patterns of borrowing in the interim. For instance, it makes no difference if a customer takes many short loans or fewer longer loans, or whether a customer takes consecutive 2-week loans, or 1-week loans on alternating weeks. All that matters is that indebtedness 90 days later is a positive indication of propensity to stay in debt.

Additionally, all simultaneous loans are combined and considered as single loans. This is done in order to facilitate comparisons in both the volume and average size of loans across regulatory regimes that allow and don't allow simultaneous borrowing.

Consistently coding state regulations themselves presents another challenge. For analytical tractability, complex regulations must necessarily be simplified and regularized. The challenge is to do this in such a way as to capture the important details and distinctions of the laws, while eliding less relevant details. Tables 2 and 3 present a simplified matrix of state payday regulations. Explanations of how regulations were interpreted to create the variables in this matrix, as well as how the information in the matrix was further coded in order to perform regression analyses, are provided in detail in Appendix A.

3.2. Regulatory Variation in the Data. The data contain regulatory variation both across states and across time. Of the two forms of variation, regulatory variation across time may be econometrically cleaner. States differ from one another in many ways unrelated to their payday lending regulations (for instance, in their other consumer protections) and these differences may impact borrowing outcomes directly. In addition, state regulation itself is likely influenced by previous borrowing outcomes. For instance suppose that, for unrelated reasons, customers in State A have greater problems with repeat borrowing than customers in State B. This may cause lawmakers in

---

[5]Ninety days is longer than any individual loan in the data, but shorter than many spells of repeat borrowing. Results are robust to using alternate follow-up periods.

State A to enact stricter laws than lawmakers in State B. These laws may themselves have some effect on outcomes, but it would be incorrect to attribute the entire difference in borrowing outcomes between the states to the difference in laws. The inclusion of macroeconomic covariates such as the local unemployment rate may help ameliorate this problem, but only partially.

In contrast, variation within state over time is likely to be less problematic. Though states that enact law changes may differ systematically from states that do not, it is likely the case that within-state before-and-after comparisons, particularly if they are focused tightly around the time of the law change, reflect the actual effects of the change in regulatory regime. Though there may be differences in usage across time for reasons unrelated to the law change, these changes a) are unlikely to be sharp discontinuities, and b) can be identified by examining trends over time in states without law changes. Econometrically we can apply a regression discontinuity design to look for sharp changes in outcomes, and a difference-in-difference design in order to difference out trends that are common to all states.

However, such a design can only identify the effect of whatever bundle of laws each state altered—there is no easy way to separate out the effect of a price cap from, say, the effect of a cooling-off period requirement if a state implemented both of these things at once. In order to separately identify the effects of components of regulation, one would ideally have many different law changes and run a pooled regression with both state and time fixed effects. However, of the states in the data, only six amended their payday lending laws in some fashion during the sample period: Ohio, Rhode Island, South Carolina, Tennessee, Virginia, and Washington.[6] Unfortunately, this is too few law changes to allow for a regression containing state fixed effects. Instead, to attempt to separately identify the impact of different components of the law we run pooled regressions with time fixed effects and macroeconomic convariates. This regression relies partially on cross-state regulatory variation.

Though without a doubt regulations are not randomly assigned to states, it is also the case that they do not follow obvious patterns. For instance, Figure 2 presents a map of the states, divided

---

[6]A seventh state, Mississippi, amended its laws in July of 2012, which while technically falling within the timeframe of the data occurred too close to the end of the sample to allow for analysis of the post-period.

according to the strigency of their price caps. High and low caps are well-distributed across the map, rather than clustering in particular regions. Figure 3 shows an equivalent map for rollover prohibitions. Law distributions such as these give one some reassurance that regressions employing cross-state regulatory variation are not hopelessly contaminated by omitted variables bias.

Though neither of these approaches (cross-state variation with time fixed effects, within-state variation due to law changes) is perfect, each corrects some of the shortcomings of the other. Cross-state regressions allow us to break apart bundles of laws, and make use a wide range of regulatory variation. Within-state law changes allow us to better control for state-specific factors and more convincingly identify the effects of the laws themselves.[7]

3.3. **Econometric Specifications.** In order to take advantage of cross-state law variation we use the following specification:

$$(1) \quad Y_i = \alpha_0 + \alpha_1 fee300_{ts} + \alpha_2 maxsize_{ts} + \alpha_3 minterm_{ts} + \alpha_4 maxterm_{ts}$$
$$+ \alpha_5 nosimult_{ts} + \alpha_6 nosimultlender_{ts} + \alpha_7 norollover_{ts} + \alpha_8 cooling_{ts} + \alpha_8 extended_{ts}$$
$$+ \alpha_9 \mathbf{M}_{ti} + \alpha_{10} \mathbf{T_t} + \nu_s + \epsilon_i$$

where Y_i is an outcome of interest such as amount borrowed, $fee300_{ts}$ and $maxsize_{ts}$ are in dollars, $minterm_{ts}$ and $maxterm_{ts}$ are in days, and the other five law variables are binary. Because the main source of variation is differences in laws across states we cannot add state fixed effects, but we can at least partially account for cross-state differences with $\mathbf{M_{ti}}$, a vector of macroeconomic variables including monthly unemployment at the state level provided by the Bureau of Labor Statistics and monthly house prices at the zip code level provided by CoreLogic. $\mathbf{T_t}$ is a set of time

---

[7]An earlier version of this paper employed a third empirical strategy: comparisons across state borders. Assuming that macroeconomic variables do not capture all relevant local variation, a borrower within, say, 25 miles of a border on one side may make a good control for a borrower within 25 miles on the other side. However, this works best for omitted variables that are likely to vary smoothly over space; omitted variables such as other state laws will also vary sharply at the border and so will not be controlled for with this method. Furthermore, there must also be a critical density of branches on both sides of the border. In the end, the border regressions were dropped due to concerns that state-specific idiosyncracies, rather than differences in payday regulations, were driving the results. They are available from the author by request.

dummies for every month in the data, v_s is a state-specific error term, and ϵ_i is the idiosyncratic error term.

For regressions in which Y_i is delinquency or repeat borrowing, both of which are binary, the regression is estimated as a probit with marginal effects reported. In all other cases it is estimated as ordinary least squares. All standard errors are clustered at the state level. For regressions in which Y_i is indebtedness three months later, the relevant law is the law in force three months later. For this reason, whenever this dependent variable is used the laws are coded to reflect the law in force at the time of the outcome, rather than the time of origination. Because in many cases the transition from one legal regime to another disrupts loans made very close to the time of the change, making them atypical of loans either before or after, all regressions are estimated removing loans made within 30 days of the change itself.

The within-state law change analyses use regressions of the following form:

(2) $$Y_i = \beta_0 + \beta_1 A_t * S_s + \beta_2 S_s + \beta_3 A_t + \beta_4 t + \beta_5 t * A_t + \beta_6 \mathbf{M_{ti}} + \beta_7 \mathbf{Q_t} + v_s + \epsilon_i$$

where A_t is a dummy variable equal to 1 if the loan was originated after the law change, S_s is a dummy variable equal to 1 if the loan was originated in the state that changed its law, t is the time running variable, and $\mathbf{Q_t}$ is a set of month dummies meant to capture seasonal factors. Y_i, $\mathbf{M_{ti}}$, v_s, and ϵ_i are the same as before. In this setting the coefficient β_1 captures the discontinuous jump at the time of the law change in the state that changed the law, with β_4 and β_5 capturing linear trends on either side of the discontinuity and β_3 capturing jumps that happen in other states at the time of the change. Again, when Y_i is delinquency or repeat borrowing the regression is estimated as a probit, and when Y_i is repeat borrowing the laws are coded to correspond to the time of the outcome rather than the time of origination.

South Carolina provides an interesting case because it had not one law change but two. The state amended its law on June 16, 2009, raising the maximum loan size to $550, creating an extended repayment option, instituting a 1-day cooling-off period between loans (2-day after the eighth loan in the calendar year) and prohibiting customers from taking more than one loan at a time. However, in order to allow time for the establishment of a statewide database the simultaneous lending and cooling-off provisions did not take effect until February 1, 2010. This delay of part of the law makes it potentially possible to separate the effects of the simultaneous lending prohibition and cooling-off period from the effects of the size limit and extended repayment option, and necessitates a slightly different specification:

$$(3) \quad Y_i = \beta_0 + \beta_1 A^1_t * S_s + \gamma_1 A^2_t * S_s + \beta_2 S_s + \beta_3 A^1_t + \gamma_3 A^2_t + \beta_4 t + \beta_5 t * A^1_t + \gamma_5 t * A^2_t + \beta_6 M_{ti} + \beta_7 Q_t + \nu_s + \epsilon_i$$

where A^1_t is a binary variable equal to 1 after the first law change, and A^2_t is a binary variable equal to 1 after the second law change. Now β_1 and γ_1 capture the effects of the first and second laws changes, respectively.

4. RESULTS

4.1. Using Cross-State Variation. Table 4 presents the results of regressions employing cross-state regulatory variation. Each column corresponds to a separate regression of the form given in Equation (1). These regressions help us understand the contributions of various regulatory components.

The first column uses fees per $100 as the dependent variable. Only two coefficients are significant: the price cap on a $300 loan, and the maximum loan size. It is easy to imagine why the price cap would matter for the price, and the coefficient of 0.25 implies that for each $1 the price cap increases, the actual price goes up 75 cents.[8] It is more difficult to see why the size cap would matter for the price. A likely explanation is that this is due to the functional form used to express the price cap in the regressions. Price caps are not single numbers; instead they tend to be price schedules, and those schedules tend to be concave in the size of the loan. In other words,

---

[8]Note that one figure is stated in terms of the fee on a $300 loan while the other is stated as an average per $100.

in many states as loans get larger the per-dollar price cap drops. Using one number for the price cap effectively assumes that all price schedules are linear. It may be that $maxsize_{ts}$ picks up the non-linearity of actual price cap schedules. It's also notable that the estimated effect is very small: an increase of 30 cents per $100 increase in the size cap.

The next column's dependent variable is total loan size. Unsuprisingly, maximum size caps matter, with an estimated increase of $41 per $100 increase in the size cap. However, this is well below the one-to-one correspondence we would see if size caps are binding. Maximum loan term and rollover prohibitions also come in as significant, though the connection is less clear.

Only one variable significantly affects loan term, and that is minimum loan term. The coefficient just misses the 5% significance mark ($p = 0.052$) and implies a 10-day increase in the minimum will raise lengths by 2.6 days on average. This effect is likely non-linear and concentrated among states with longer minimum loan terms. Notably, the estimate for maximum term is insignificant and economically small, suggesting it rarely if ever binds.

Price caps and size caps are the only types of regulation that are significantly predictive of delinquency, with coefficients implying that a $10 increase in the cap on a $300 loan increases delinquency by 0.6 percentage points, and a $100 increase in the size cap increases delinquency by 0.4 percentage points. These effects are moderate relative to an overall delinquency rate of 4.3%, and the mechanism by which they might affect the rate is not certain. One possibility is that larger and more expensive loans are simply more difficult to pay off, leading to delinquency.

Four types of regulation appear predictive of repeat borrowing: price caps, maximum term limits, rollover prohibitions, and cooling-off periods. It is easy to see why there might be a connection between rollover prohibitions and cooling-off periods—both are specifically designed to limit repeat borrowing, and indeed both coefficients are significant and negative. Though much of the debate over rollover prohibitions focuses on the ability of lenders and borrowers to circumvent them, it is possible that on the margin such prohibitions still make rollovers a bit less convenient, with consequences for overall repeat borrowing.

It is less straightforward to see the link between price caps and repeat borrowing. The coefficient implies a significant 3 percentage point decrease in the repeat borrowing rate for each $10 increase in the cap. One possibility is that this is a simple price effect: cheaper loans are more attractive to prospective customers and so they choose to use them more often. Another possibility is that, assuming higher price caps lead to greater delinquency, delinquent borrowers are less likely to be allowed to borrow in the future, leading to less repeat borrowing. However, the estimated effect of price caps on repeat borrowing is larger than the estimated effect on delinquency, suggesting this cannot be the sole mechanism.

Lastly, maximum loan term is negatively associated with repeat borrowing. Given that this form of regulation appears to have no effect on loan term itself, its putative target, it is difficult to imagine a channel by which it would affect repeat borrowing.

4.2. **Using Variation from Law Changes.** Next we examine states that changed their laws in order to see whether the results obtained from the pooled regressions of the previous section are supported or contradicted in a setting with fewer confounding factors. Table 5 presents analyses of the six states in the data with law changes. Each cell of the table represents a separate regression using the specification in Equation (2), except for the South Carolina cells which use the specification in Equation (3). For reference, Figures 4, 5, 6, 7, 8, and 9 present raw means over time for fees, amount borrowed, loan term, lending volume, delinquency, and repeat borrowing for each state whose laws changed.[9]

The pooled regressions suggested a fairly tight connection between price caps and price, and this relationship appears at least as strong in the law-change regressions. As noted in the law matrix in Tables 2 and 3, price caps went up in Ohio and Rhode Island, while Tennessee and Virginia both loosened theirs. All four states saw price changes in the direction of the price cap changes, and the sizes of the price changes closely track the size of the cap changes: $1.03, 96 cents, 56 cents, and $1.16 changes per $1 change in the cap, respectively. The remaining states did not adjust their price caps, and their prices did not change. These results support the conclusion that actual prices adhere closely to price caps.

---

[9]The figures reveal significant seasonal cycles for some variables, notably delinquency and repeat borrowing, though the seasonal factors in the regressions ensure these cycles don't contaminate the law change estimates. This seasonality stems largely from tax returns: many people use their returns as a lump sum payment to retire their loans, causing temporary decreases in rates of delinquency and repeat borrowing.

The connection between loan size limits and loan size appears weaker in the law-change regressions than it did in the pooled regressions. Ohio's limit increased but its loan size did not, while Tennessee's limit and loan size actually went in opposite directions. South Carolina's loan size may have increased slightly when it raised its limit, only to decrease again when it added its simultaneous loan prohibition (Table 5 shows a marginally-significant $27 increase, though there is no observable jump in Figure 6). The lack of connection between legal limit and amount borrowed may be because, unlike price caps, size caps are often not low enough to be binding on lenders.

The pooled regressions found no relationship between simultaneous borrowing prohibitions and total amount borrowed even though amount borrowed, as contructed, merged simultaneous loans together. The law-change regressions support a similar conclusion. Ohio removed its simultaneous borrowing limit, while Virginia instituted a new limit, neither of which appears to have affected total amount borrowed. The result is particularly notable for South Carolina, which prior to its changes had a single-loan size limit of $300. Approximately 71.5% of all its loans were made simultaneously with at least one other loan, for an average borrowing amount of about $420. After the first law change the single-loan limit increased to $500 but simultaneous loans were still legal, effectively making it easier to borrow much larger amounts. However, the total amount borrowed rose only slightly. After the second change simultaneous loans became illegal, and dropped to only 2.4% of loan volume. Average single-loan size increased, leaving total amount borrowed largely unchanged. Overall, it appears that customers were able to borrow the desired amount no matter whether the limit was structured as a size cap or a simultaneous borrowing ban. This suggests that unless states enact much more binding limits on the maximum amount borrowed it may not matter whether or not they also have limits on simultaneous borrowing.

The pooled regressions found that minimum loan terms affect loan length, and the law-change results support that. Only one state changed its laws regarding minimum or maximum loan term: Virginia raised its minimum loan term from 7 days to two times the length of the borrower's pay cycle. Assuming a standard pay cycle of two weeks, this raises the effective limit by about 21 days. The third column of Table 5 estimates that loan length in Virginia increased nearly 20 days on average as a result, suggesting that the change was binding. OH and WA both exhibit more modest changes in average loan term, though neither directly changed their loan term regulations and Ohio's change was not statistically significant.

All six states saw statistically significant changes in their rates of loan delinquency. The largest change occurred in Virginia, where delinquency rose nearly 7 percentage points over a base rate of about 4%. The law-change evidence shows a connection between price caps and delinquency, consistent with the pooled regressions. Price caps and delinquency alike dropped in Ohio and Rhode Island, while price caps and delinquency rose in Tennessee and Virginia. The connection between size caps and delinquency found in the pooled regressions gets notably less support: the three states that changed their size caps saw delinquency move in the wrong direction or not at all.

The rate of repeat borrowing also changed in all six states, though the change was large in only four of them. Ohio's rate increased about 14 percentage points, while South Carolina, Virginia, and Washington decreased their rates by 15, 26, and 33 percentage points, respectively. The pooled regressions indicated that repeat borrowing should decrease with the implementation of rollover prohibitions and cooling-off provisions. Unfortunately no state changed its rollover prohibition so the law-change regressions can provide no evidence either way. South Carolina, Virginia, and Washington all instituted cooling-off provisions and all saw large decreases in repeat borrowing, supporting the pooled regressions. South Carolina in particular saw its largest decrease after its second regulatory change, when it instituted its cooling-off provision. Washington implemented a strict 8-loan per year limit on lending, which can be thought of as an unusual form of cooling-off provision, and saw the largest repeat borrowing decrease of all.

The pooled regressions also suggested that higher fee caps lowered repeat borrowing, and this too gets further support. The two states that raised their fee caps, Tennessee and Virginia, saw drops in repeat borrowing while the two states where they decreased, Ohio and Rhode Island, saw jumps. Though the pooled regressions showed no relationship, the two states that instituted simultaneous borrowing prohibitions, South Carolina and Virginia, saw big drops in repeat borrowing, while Ohio, whose simultaneous borrowing ban was rendered obsolete when lenders began to lend under a new statute, saw a big increase in repeat borrowing.

Taking a step back it appears that three states—South Carolina, Virginia, and Washington—enacted changes that had large effects on lending within their borders. For Washington the key provision may have been the 8-loan maximum, and for Virginia, the unusually long minimum loan term. South Carolina changed many smaller things at once. All three states saw their rates of repeat borrowing plummet. The changes were disruptive: Virginia and Washington, and to a lesser extent South Carolina, all saw large drops in total lending.[10] Besides being an interesting outcome in its own right, the change in lending volume suggests that customer composition may have changed as well.

Without demographic data it is difficult to assess changes in composition. Table 6 attempts to get a handle on the question by asking how often customers who were repeat borrowers prior to the law change appear in the data after the law change. Customers are divided according to whether their pre-period loans led to indebtedness a greater or smaller proportion of the time than was the median for all pre-period borrowers. A borrower is considered to appear in the post-period if he or she takes any loan in the post-period. Naturally, repeat borrowers are more likely to appear in the post-period no matter what the regulatory environment, so similar figures are computed for customers in other states in order to get a baseline. The rightmost column presents odds ratios, with numbers 1 indicating the degree to which pre-period repeat borrowers are over-represented in the post-period.

As expected, the data show that repeat borrowers are much more likely to show up than occasional borrowers in the post-period in all states. The odds ratio for Virginia is much lower than for other states, suggesting that in Virginia the law change significantly altered customer composition. In South Carolina and Washington, however, the odds ratios look more normal. Both states were marginally more likely than other states to retain non-repeat borrowers, but the differences

---

[10]Loans from a single lender are, in general, ill suited to estimating the effects of regulation on total lending volume. The lender may have greater pentration in some states than others, and may expand or contract operations for reasons unrelated to the legal environment. However, there is reason to believe these particular drops in volume are due to the law changes themselves. These drops do not correspond to mass branch closings, but instead to decreases in loans per branch. In both Virginia and Washington the lender did eventually close many branches, but this appears to be a consequence rather than a cause of the drop in volume. South Carolina never had any mass closings.

are small, suggesting that these states did not experience notable customer selection when lending volume dropped.

Finally, as in the pooled regressions, the law-change results show no evidence that extended repayment options matter. This may be due to the omission of Colorado, the only state where extended repayment is mandatory, not just an option. It may also be due to the fact that the lender providing the data makes extended repayment options available even in states that don't require it. As such, these regressions may not capture the impact of extended repayment options on lenders without such a policy.

5. CONCLUSIONS

Overall, pooled cross-state regressions and within-state regressions examining law changes show a remarkable amount of agreement. Both suggest the following conclusions about payday lending regulation: price caps tend to be strictly binding, size caps tend to be less binding, and prohibitions on simultaneous borrowing appear to have little effect on the total amount borrowed. Minimum term limits affect loan length, but maximum term limits do not. Delinquency seems positively related to higher price caps. Rollover prohibitions and cooling-off periods, as well as to higher price caps, appear to reduce the frequency of repeat borrowing.

Focusing on states with law changes, South Carolina, Virginia, and Washington were all able to significantly cut their rates of repeat borrowing. These changes were accompanied by significant upheavals, however, particularly in Virginia and Washington where loan volume dropped sharply and, in the case of Virginia, delinquency spiked and customer composition shifted. It seems likely that Virginia's changes were connected to its adoption of a 2-pay-period minimum term, which is longer than the minimum term of most states. It will be interesting to follow what happens in Mississippi, which like Virginia recently adopted a long minimum term limit. Washington's changes seem plausibly related to its adoption of an 8-loan yearly maximum, another form of regulation unusual among states. In South Carolina the decline in repeat borrowing is less readily pinned on a single provision.

This paper has attempted to get inside the monolith of payday lending and examine how different regulatory environments affect loan terms and usage. Without a doubt there remains greater detail to explore—for instance, both cooling-off provisions and extended repayment options vary greatly across states. It is possible that particular instances of these regulations, like for instance those adopted by South Carolina, might have effects on delinquency or repeat borrowing that are not captured by the average effect of all laws in that regulatory category. In the face of state-specific idiosyncracies, however, the more fine-grained the question the more challenging it is to move beyond informed speculation.

Payday lending is not one product but many. The price, size, and duration of payday loans, as well as the manner in which customers use them, varies greatly according to their regulatory environment. As we possibly move toward a regime of federal regulation, it is crucial to better understand how these different types of regulation work.

References

AVERY, R., AND K. SAMOLYK (2011): "Payday Loans versus Pawnshops: The Effects of Loan Fee Limits on Household Use," *Working paper*.

BHUTTA, N., P. SKIBA, AND J. TOBACMAN (2012): "Payday Loan Choices and Consequences," *Vanderbilt University Law & Economics Working Paper no. 12-30*.

CARRELL, S., AND J. ZINMAN (2013): "In Harm's Way? Payday Loan Access and Military Personnel Performance," *Working paper*.

CASKEY, J. (1996): *Fringe Banking: Check-Cashing Outlets, Pawnshops, and the Poor*. The Russell Sage Foundation.

ELLIEHAUSEN, G. (2009): "An Analysis of Consumers' Use of Payday Loans," *Financial Services Research Program Monograph, no. 41*.

FDIC (2013): "Addendum to the 2011 FDIC National Survey of Unbanked and Underbanked Households: Use of Alternative Financial Services," *Federal Deposit Insurance Corporation*.

FLANNERY, M., AND K. SAMOLYK (2007): "Scale Economies at Payday Loan Stores," *Working paper*.

FUSARO, M., AND P. CIRILLO (2011): "Do Payday Loans Trap Consumers in a Cycle of Debt?," *Working paper*.

GRAVES, S., AND C. PETERSON (2008): "Usury Law and The Christian Right: Faith-Based Political Power and the Geography of American Payday Loan Regulation," *Catholic University Law Review*, 57(3).

MANN, R., AND J. HAWKINS (2007): "Just Until Payday," *UCLA Law Review*, 54(4), 855–912.

MELZER, B. (2011): "The Real Costs of Credit Access: Evidence from the Payday Lending Market," *Quarterly Journal of Economics*, 126, 517–555.

MORGAN, D., AND M. STRAIN (2008): "Payday Holiday: How Households Fare after Payday Credit Bans," *Federal Reserve Bank of New York Staff Reports, no. 309*.

MORSE, A. (2011): "Payday Lenders: Heroes or Villians?," *Journal of Financial Economics*, 102, 28–44.

PARRISH, L., AND U. KING (2009): "Phantom Demand: Short-term due date generates need for repeat payday loans, accounting for 76% of total volume," *Center for Responsible Lending*.

PEW CHARITABLE TRUSTS (2012): "Who Borrows, Where They Borrow, and Why," *Payday Lending in America*.

STEGMAN, M. (2007): "Payday Lending," *Journal of Economic Perspectives*, 21(1), 169–190.

STEPHENS INC. (2011): "Payday Loan Industry," *Industry Report*.

APPENDIX A

Notes on coding by type of regulation.

Price caps. For analytical tractability this paper collapses complex fee schedules into a single number: the dollar limit on fees for a hypothetical $300 loan. For example, Indiana limits fees to 15% of the first $250 lent, 13% of the next $251-$400, and 10% of anything above that. In this case the fee for a $300 loan would be $0.15*250+0.13*50 = \$44$. All caps are considered inclusive of database fees, verification fees, and other add-on fees. States without any price cap are treated as if they had a cap equal to the highest cap of any state in the data, which is the $73.52 cap for Virginia after January 1, 2009.

Size caps. States vary according to whether their size cap is stated inclusive of exclusive of fees. For comparability, this paper codes all size caps as if they were exclusive of fees. In other words, if a state limits loan size to $500 inclusive of fees, as for instance Nebraska does, this is coded as an exclusive size limit of $425 because $75 has gone to fees. (Technically a lender in Nebraska could offer a loan with principal higher than $425 if its fees were set below the state statuatory maximum, but in practice lenders tend to charge the maximum allowed.) For states that set their size cap as the minimum of an absolute size limit and a percentage of the borrower's monthly limit I assume an annual income of $31,000, which is the median annual income of payday loan borrowers in the 2010 Survey of Consumer Finances. Using this income level, monthly income limits are not binding for any state. States with no size caps are coded as having a cap equal to the cap in the state with the highest cap, which is $1000 for Idaho.

Minimum term limits. For states that set the minimum term limit in terms of pay periods rather than days, a standard pay period of 2 weeks is assumed. For instance, Virginia's limit of 2 pay periods is coded as 28 days.

Maximum term limits. States with no maximum term limits are coded as having a limit equal to the state with the highest legal limit, which is 60 days for Kentucky.

Limits on simultaneous borrowing. Simultaneous borrowing limits are divided into two variables: the limit on absolute number of loans, and the limit of the number of loans per lender. In regression analysis both of these are collapsed into binary variables. These variables take the value 1 if the state limits customers to one loan at a time, and 0 otherwise. This means that states limiting customers to two or more loans at a time are considered equivalent to states with no limit. This decision was made in light of the fact that in states with no limit it is rare to borrow more than two loans at a time; therefore, a limit of two loans is unlikely to be binding on many customers.

Rollover prohibitions. For states in which the rollover limit is stated in weeks rather than in the number of renewals, 2 weeks is considered equivalent to 1 renewal. In regression analysis the rollover variable is collapsed into a binary equal to 1 if rollovers are completely prohibited, and 0 if some form of rollover is allowed (even if it requires part of the principle to be paid down). Note that an alternate definition, considering paydown-only rollovers as equivalent to rollover prohibitions, yields empirical results very similar to the results presented in the paper.

Cooling-off periods. Cooling-off periods are stated in days. Given variability in both the length of cooling-off periods and in the conditions under which they are triggered, in regression analysis they are collapsed into a binary variable equal to 1 if the state employs some type of cooling-off regulation, and 0 otherwise.

Extended repayment options. Extended repayment options are extremely variable both in their form and in the conditions under which they are triggered. In regression analysis they are collapsed into a binary variable equal to 1 if the state employs some type of extended repayment option, and 0 otherwise.

Notes on coding by state.

California. Calculating California's price cap per $300 is a challenge because the state has a $300 loan size cap that is inclusive of the fee. This means that if a lender were to charge the statuatory maximum of 15% of the face value of the check, or $45, the principal would be limited to $255. Lenders could make a loan with $300 principal, but it would need to have no fee. In order to calculate the per-$300 maximum fee for comparison with other states I calculate the percentage fee allowed on $255 then apply that percentage to $300. This yields $(45/255) * 300 = \$52.94$.

Ohio. The Ohio Short Term Loan Act, meant to govern payday lending, sets an APR cap of 28%, effectively making payday lending impossible. However, lenders have circumvented the Act by lending under either the Ohio Small Loan Act or, more commonly, the Ohio Mortgage Lending Act. Because the Short Term Loan Act is irrelevent to lending in the state, this coding uses values derived from the Mortgage Lending Act.

Tennessee. Tennessee allows a maximum of two loans simultaneously, and they cannot sum to an amount greater than $500. Given that $500 is also the size limit for a single loan, the dollar limit will bind more strongly that the limit on the number of simultaneous loans, making the effective loan limit 1. Tennessee has a further complication in that it is the only state with a limit on the absolute number of loans per borrower, but no database through which lenders can check for other outstanding loans. This lack of an enforcement mechanism effectively renders the absolute loan limit moot. Hence, even though on the books both the absolute and lender-specific limits are 2, in practice I have coded them as "no limit" and 1, respectively.

Washington. Washington uses a form of regulation that is unique among states in the data: an absolute limit of 8 loans per customer per year. This regulation most closely resembles a cooling-off period, in that it could be considered a permanent cooling-off period triggered after the 8th loan. For this reason I've coded Washington's cooling-off variable as 1, though the regulation is different enough from other cooling-off regulation to merit consideration in its own right.

APPENDIX B

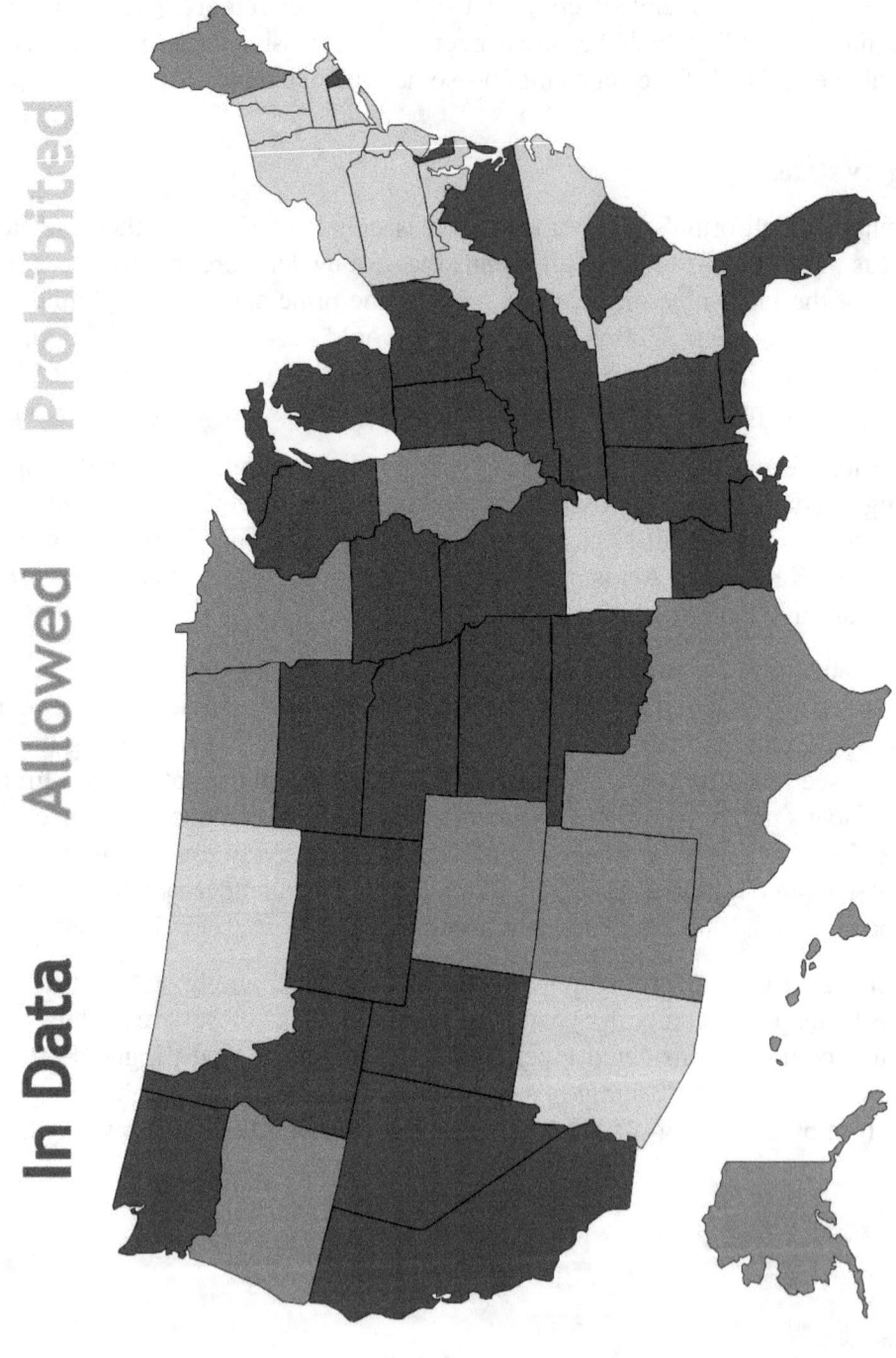

FIGURE 1. States in the data are shown in dark blue, states that allow payday lending but are not in the data are shown in medium blue, and states that prohibit payday lending are shown in light blue.

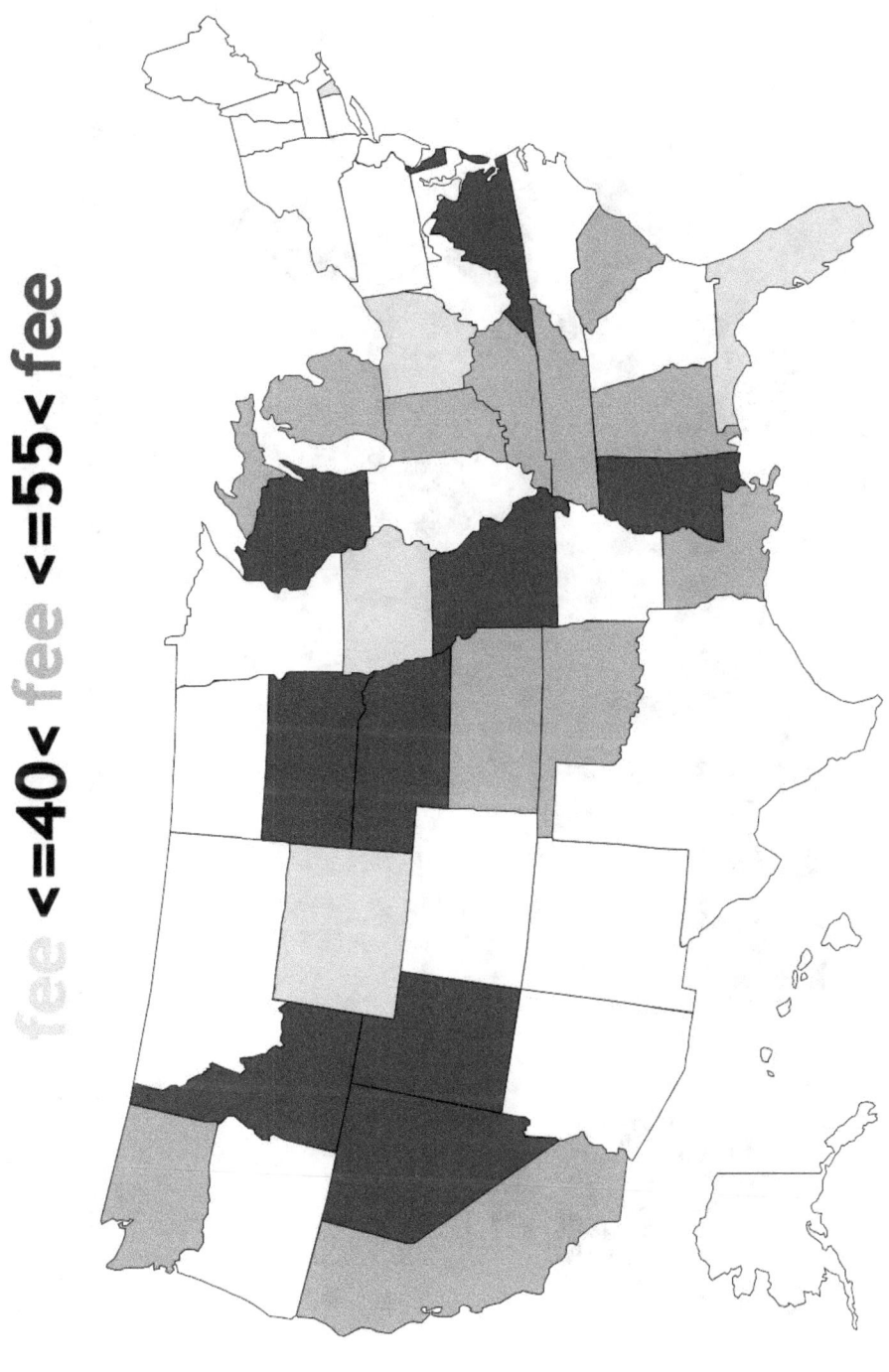

FIGURE 2. States in the data with fee caps per $300 greater than $55 are shown in dark green, with caps greater than $40 and less than or equal to $55 are shown in medium green, and with caps less than or equal to $40 are shown in light green.

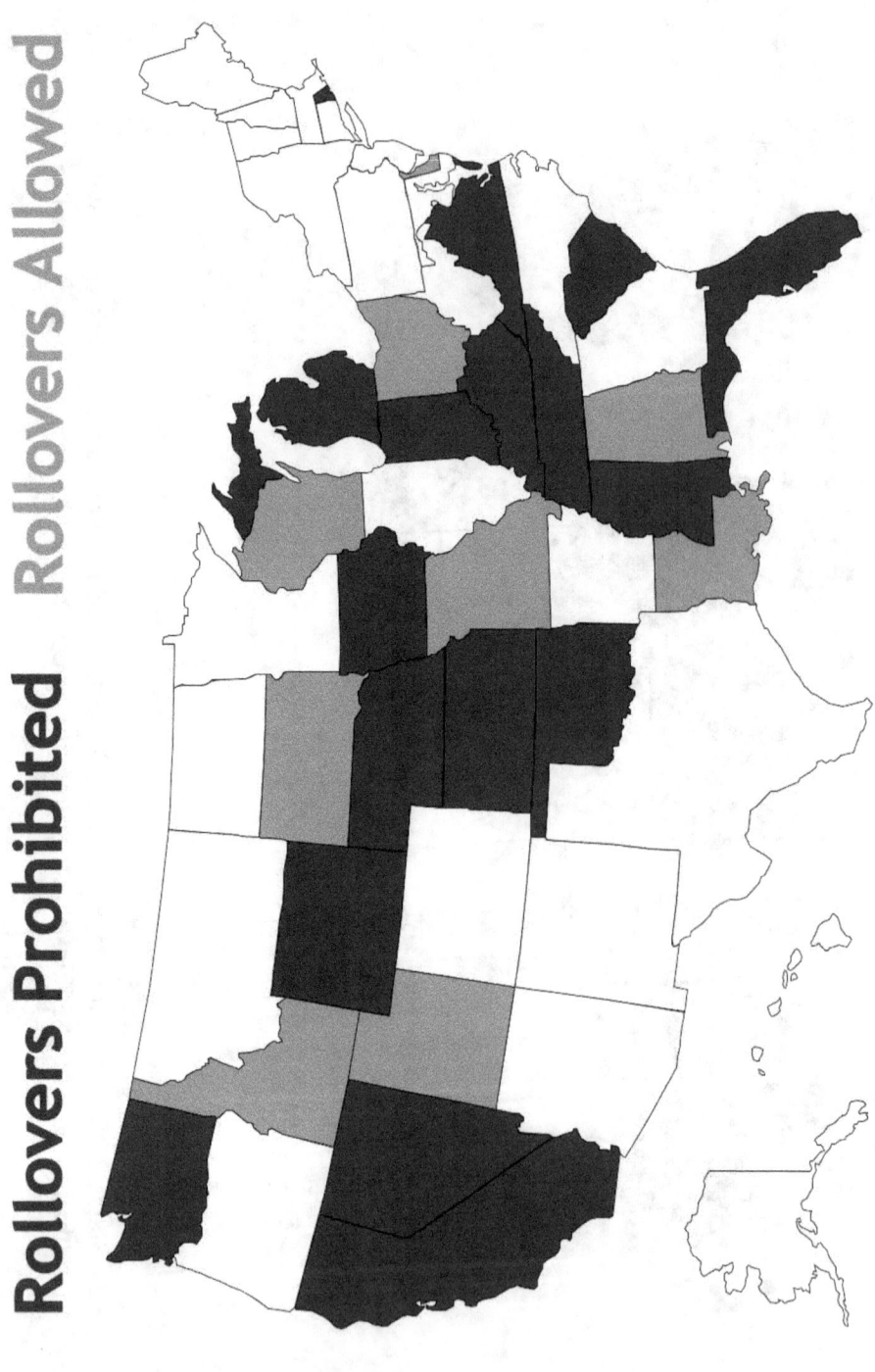

FIGURE 3. States in the data that prohibit all rollovers are shown in dark purple, and those that allow some form of rollovers are shown in light purple.

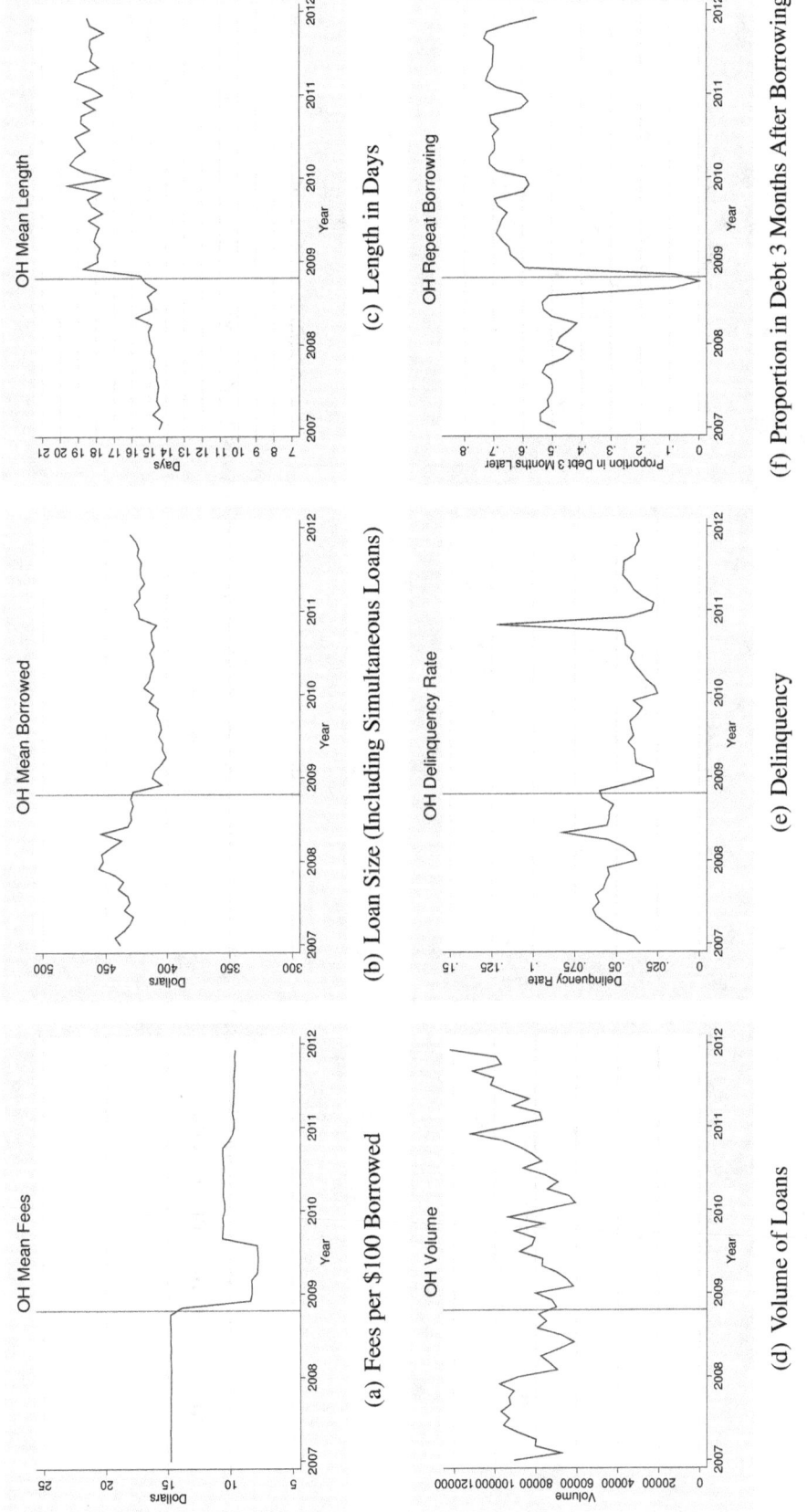

FIGURE 4. Ohio: fees, loan size, loan term, volume, delinquency, and repeat borrowing. Vertical red line represents timing of law change.

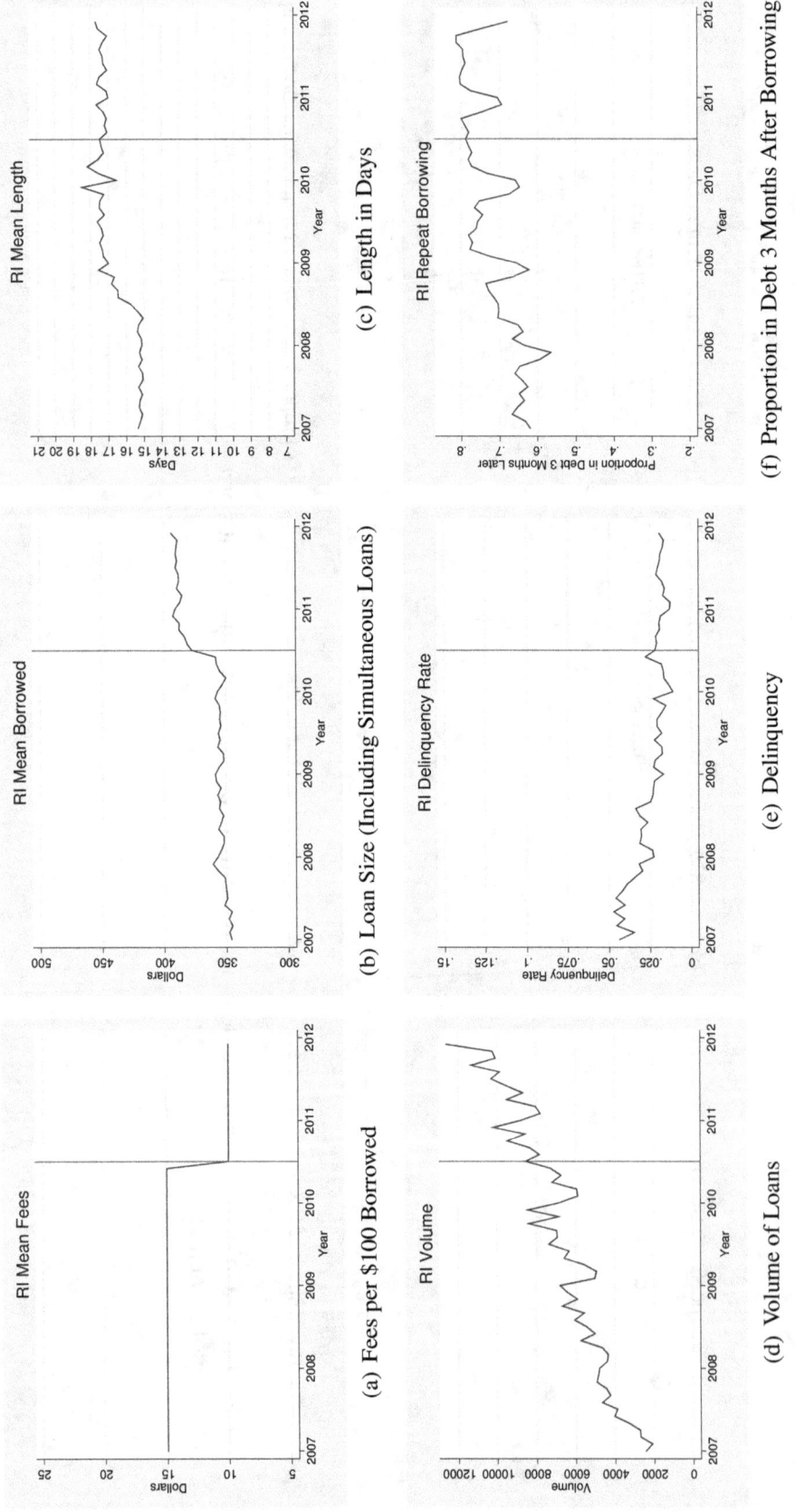

FIGURE 5. Rhode Island: fees, loan size, loan term, volume, delinquency, and repeat borrowing. Vertical red line represents timing of law change.

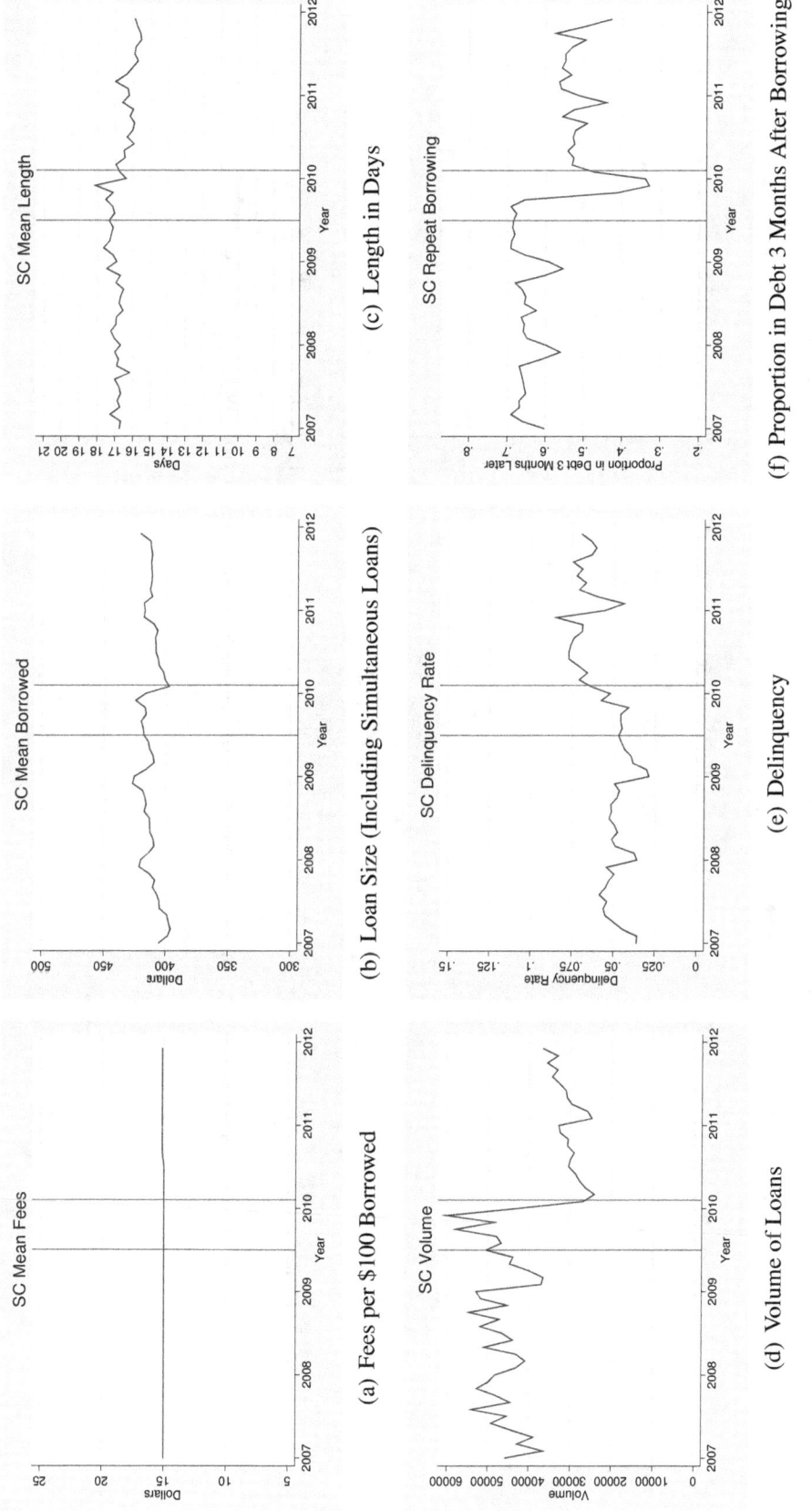

FIGURE 6. South Carolina: fees, loan size, loan term, volume, delinquency, and repeat borrowing. Vertical red lines represent timing of law changes.

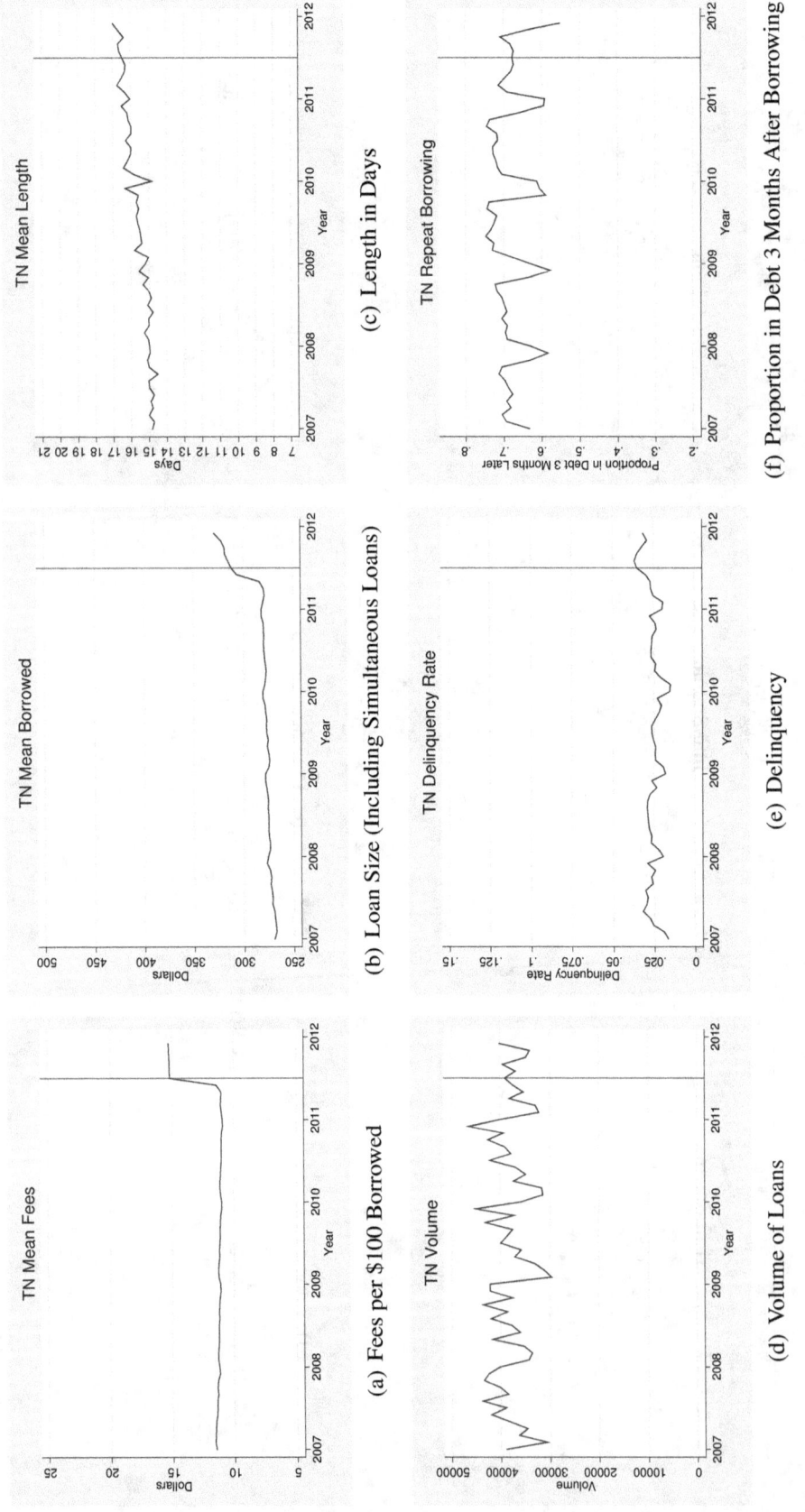

FIGURE 7. Tennessee: fees, loan size, loan term, volume, delinquency, and repeat borrowing. Vertical red line represents timing of law change.

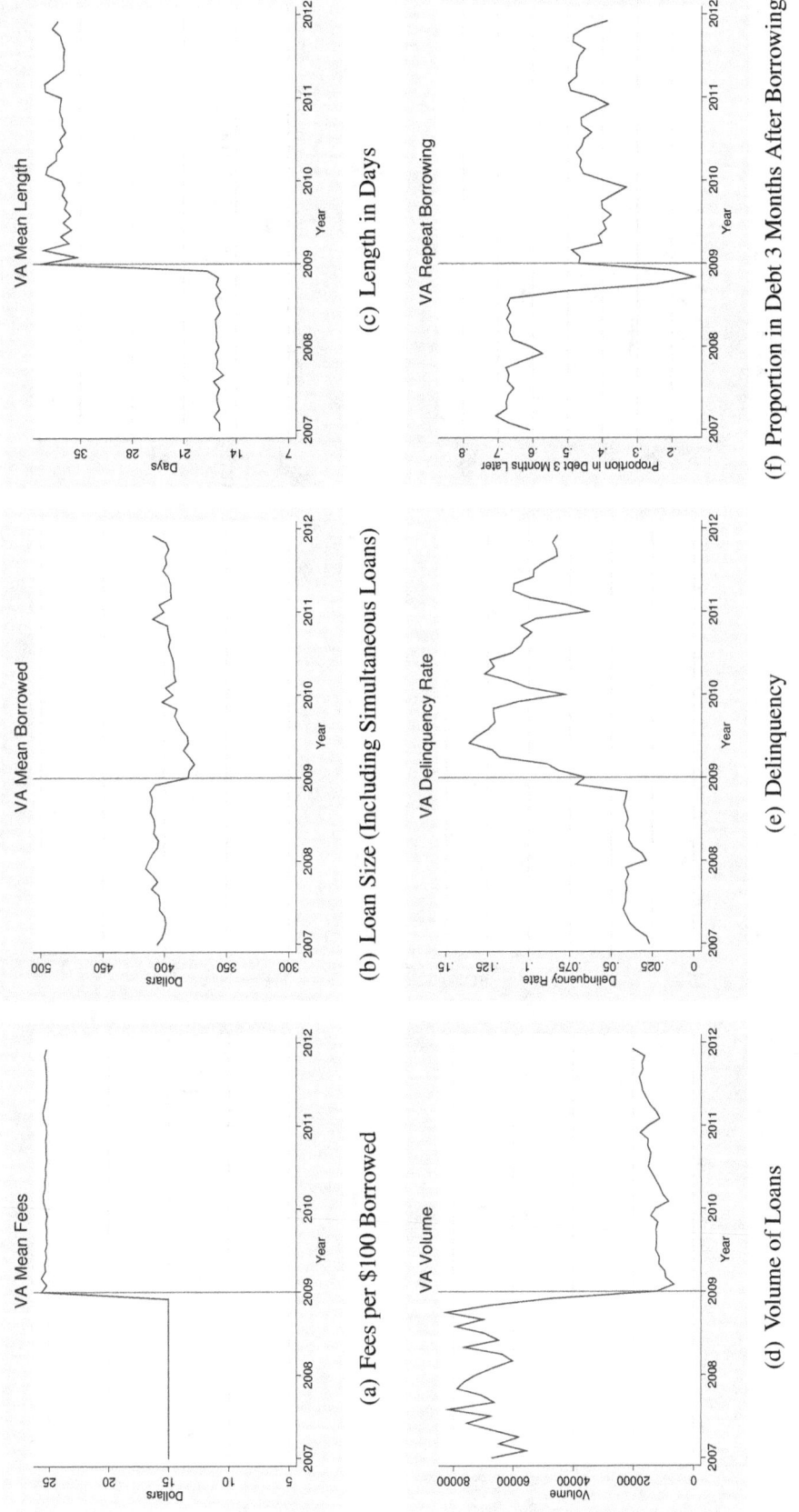

FIGURE 8. Virginia: fees, loan size, loan term, volume, delinquency, and repeat borrowing. Vertical red line represents timing of law change.

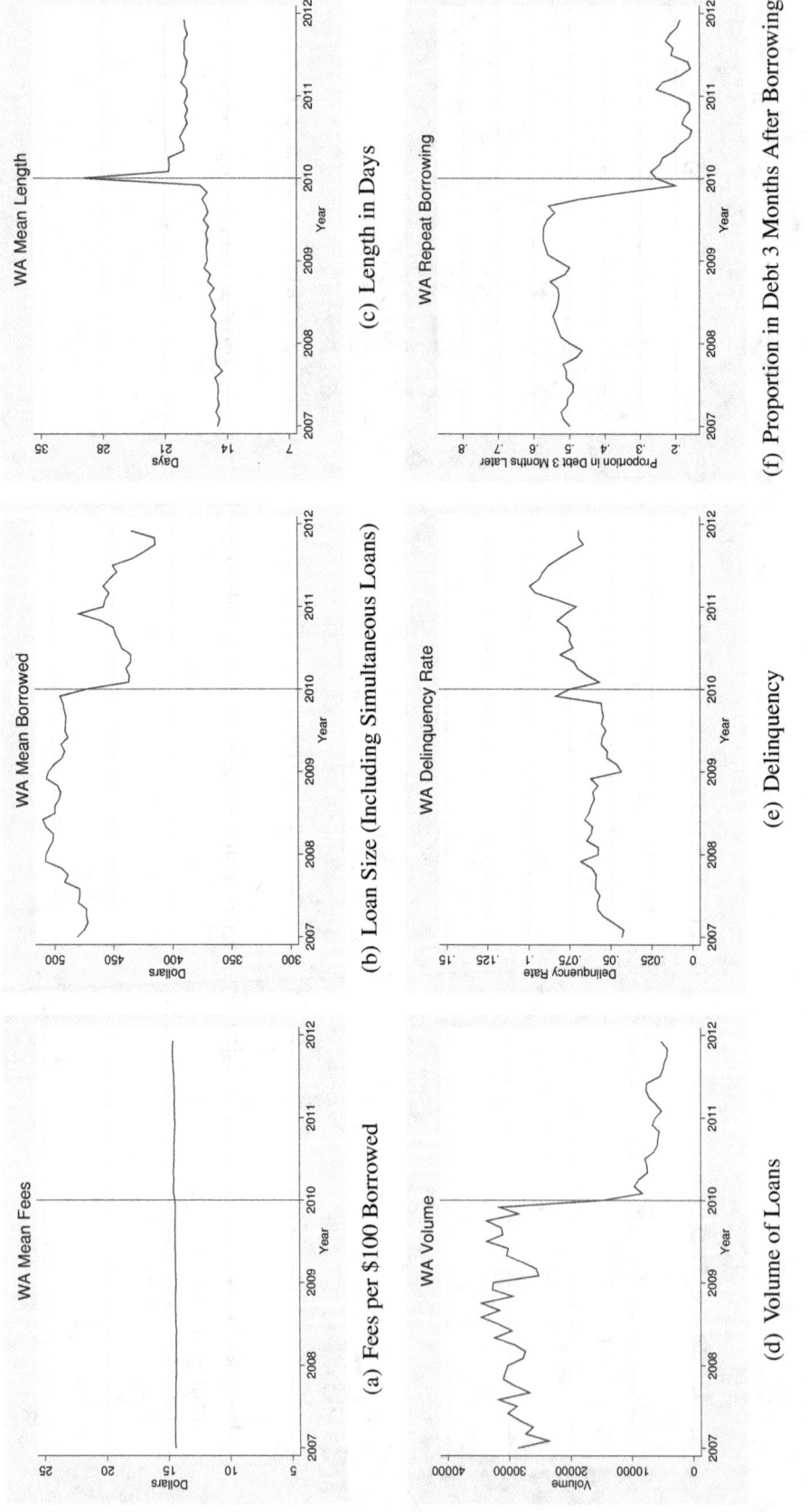

FIGURE 9. Washington: fees, loan size, loan term, volume, delinquency, and repeat borrowing. Vertical red line represents timing of law change.

TABLE 1. Summary Statistics

	Percentiles					Mean
	10%	25%	50%	75%	90%	
Total borrowed at once ($N = 54,119,468$)	$200	$255	$350	$500	$501	$370.50
Total fees at once ($N = 54,119,468$)	$29.07	$38.75	$47.95	$65.45	$85	$53.27
Loan term in days ($N = 54,119,468$)	11	13	14	18	29	16.7
APR ($N = 54,119,468$)	185.3	252.6	365	465.25	547.5	376.1
Is a repeat loan ($N = 54,119,468$)	-	-	-	-	-	86.0%
Is a simultaneous loan ($N = 54,119,468$)	-	-	-	-	-	3.6%
Delinquent ($N = 53,677,124$)	-	-	-	-	-	4.3%
Indebted 3 months later ($N = 54,119,468$)	-	-	-	-	-	57.2%
Consecutive loans after a new loan ($N = 7,571,675$)	0	0	2	7	16	5.9
Consecutive loans after any loan ($N = 54,119,468$)	0	2	6	15	30	11.5
Total loans per customer in data ($N = 3,428,271$)	1	2	7	21	43	15.8

Notes: Simultaneous loans are combined and treated as single loans, bringing the sample size from over 56 million down to just over 54 million. "Repeat/consecutive" loan defined as any loan originated less than 31 days after the previous loan was due. "New" loan defined as any loan that is not a repeat loan.

TABLE 2. Matrix of State Payday Lending Regulations

State	Fee per $300 ($)	Max Size ($)	Min Term (days)	Max Term (days)	# Simult Loans	# Simult Per Lender	# Rollovers Allowed	Cooling (days)	Extended Option	Dates
AL	52.5	500	10	31	1	1	1	1	yes	1/07–8/12
CA	52.94	255	0	31	no limit	1	0	0	yes	1/07–8/12
DE	no limit	500	0	59	no limit	no limit	4	0	no	1/07–8/12
FL	35	500	7	31	1	1	0	1	yes	1/07–8/12
IA	38.75	445	0	31	no limit	2	0	1	yes	1/07–8/12
ID	no limit	1000	0	no limit	no limit	no limit	3	0	no	1/07–8/12
IN	44	550	14	no limit	1	1	0	7	yes	1/07–8/12
KS	45	500	7	30	no limit	2	0	0	no	1/07–8/12
KY	53.94	500	14	60	1	1	0	0	no	1/07–8/12
LA	50	350	0	30	no limit	no limit	if paydown	0	no	1/07–8/12
MI	42.45	600	0	31	2	1	0	0	yes	1/07–8/12
MO	no limit	500	14	31	no limit	2	6 if paydown	0	no	1/07–8/12
MS	54	338.98	0	30	no limit	no limit	0	0	no	1/07–6/12
	65.85	414	28	30	no limit	no limit	0	0	no	7/12–8/12
NE	52.9	425	0	34	no limit	2	0	0	no	1/07–8/12
NV	no limit	625	0	35	no limit	1	5	0	yes	1/07–8/12
OH	45	800	0	no limit	no limit	1	no limit	0	no	1/07–9/08
	28.53	no limit	0	no limit	no limit	no limit	no limit	0	no	10/08–8/12
OK	45.46	500	12	45	2	2	0	2	yes	1/07–8/12
RI	45	500	13	no limit	no limit	3	1	0	no	1/07–6/10
	30	500	13	no limit	no limit	3	1	0	no	7/10–8/12
SC	45	300	0	31	no limit	no limit	0	0	no	1/07–6/15/09
	45.4	550	0	31	no limit	no limit	0	0	yes	6/16/09–1/10
	45.4	550	0	31	1	1	0	1	yes	2/10–8/12

Notes: See Appendix A.

TABLE 3. Matrix of State Payday Lending Regulations (cont'd)

State	Fee per $300 ($)	Max Size ($)	Min Term (days)	Max Term (days)	# Simult Loans	# Simult Per Lender	# Rollovers Allowed	Cooling (days)	Extended Option	Dates
SD	no limit	500	0	no limit	no limit	no limit	4 if paydown	0	no	1/07–8/12
TN	30	470	0	31	no limit	1	0	0	no	1/07–5/19/11
	52.94	425	0	31	no limit	1	0	0	no	5/20/11–8/12
UT	no limit	no limit	0	no limit	no limit	no limit	5	0	yes	1/07–8/12
VA	45	500	7	no limit	no limit	no limit	0	0	no	1/07–12/08
	73.52	500	2 pay periods	no limit	1	1	0	1	yes	1/09–8/12
WA	45	700	1 pay period	45	no limit	no limit	0	0	no	1/07–12/09
	45	700	1 pay period	45	no limit	no limit	0	rest of year	yes	1/10–8/12
WI	no limit	875	0	no limit	1	1	1	1	yes	1/07–8/12
WY	30	no limit	0	31	no limit	no limit	0	0	no	1/07–8/12

Notes: See Appendix A.

TABLE 4. Regressions Using Cross-State Law Variation

		Fee per $100 ($)	Loan Size ($)	Loan Term (days)	Delinquency (percentage points)	Repeat Borrowing (percentage points)
fee300	α_1	0.25***	0.45	0.03	0.06***	-0.30***
	s.e.	(0.03)	(0.86)	(0.05)	(0.01)	(0.09)
maxsize	α_2	-0.003**	0.41***	0.00	0.004***	-0.01
	s.e.	(0.001)	(0.07)	(0.00)	(0.001)	(0.01)
minterm	α_3	-0.05	2.37*	0.26*	0.01	0.02
	s.e.	(0.06)	(1.31)	(0.12)	(0.04)	(0.02)
maxterm	α_4	0.03	-2.66**	0.04	-0.02	-2.24**
	s.e.	(0.02)	(1.14)	(0.04)	(0.02)	(1.00)
nosimult	α_5	0.91	24.12	-1.15	-0.48	6.09
	s.e.	(0.80)	(39.0)	(1.22)	(0.64)	(5.26)
nosimultlender	α_6	0.05	-51.8	0.18	-0.11	-1.73
	s.e.	(0.73)	(45.9)	(1.46)	(0.67)	(4.17)
norollover	α_7	0.47	46.5**	-0.02	-0.54	-6.96***
	s.e.	(0.78)	(18.6)	(0.86)	(0.36)	(2.48)
cooling	α_8	-0.67	17.3	-0.83	0.45	-9.42**
	s.e.	(0.42)	(43.3)	(0.73)	(0.55)	(4.75)
extended	α_9	-0.02	14.4	1.24	0.26	-0.14
	s.e.	(0.65)	(45.0)	(0.86)	(0.49)	(0.02)
N		51,453,347	51,453,347	51,453,347	51,453,347	51,453,347

Notes: Each column is a separate regression using the specification in Equation (1). Delinquency and Repeat Borrowing are probit regressions; the rest are ordinary least squares. Regressions have controls for macroeconomic factors and dummies for every month, and have standard errors clustered at the state level. * denotes significance at the 10% level, ** denotes significance at the 5% level, and *** denotes significance at the 1% level.

TABLE 5. Regressions Using Law Changes

State		Fee per $100 ($)	Loan Size ($)	Loan Term (days)	Delinquency (percentage points)	Repeat Borrowing (percentage points)	Date of Change
OH	β_1	-5.66***	-7.48	1.53	-1.11***	13.93***	10/1/08
	s.e.	(0.57)	(15.55)	(0.98)	(0.26)	(1.74)	
	N	52,438,197	52,438,197	52,438,197	51,995,853	52,517,401	
RI	β_1	-4.80***	35.34***	-0.04	-0.63***	4.11***	7/1/10
	s.e.	(0.44)	(11.54)	(0.22)	(0.13)	(1.33)	
	N	52,664,162	52,664,162	52,664,162	52,221,818	52,864,431	
SC	β_1	-0.01	26.75*	-0.55	0.28	-2.04	6/16/09
	s.e.	(0.55)	(15.43)	(0.34)	(0.26)	(1.90)	
	γ_1	0.19	-20.69**	-2.01***	1.34***	-15.33***	2/1/10
	s.e.	(0.26)	(9.61)	(0.27)	(1.65)	(0.58)	
	N	51,265,352	51,265,352	51,265,352	50,823,008	51,294,052	
TN	β_1	4.32***	44.80***	0.15	1.73***	-6.76***	5/20/11
	s.e.	(0.41)	(7.49)	(0.46)	(0.24)	(1.49)	
	N	52,616,436	52,616,436	52,616,436	52,174,092	52,769,402	
VA	β_1	11.00***	-26.20***	19.75***	6.87***	-25.83***	1/1/09
	s.e.	(0.66)	(8.40)	(0.37)	(0.36)	(1.71)	
	N	52,517,137	52,517,137	52,517,137	52,074,793	52,395,448	
WA	β_1	0.47	-60.74***	1.87***	2.76***	-32.73***	1/1/10
	s.e.	(0.45)	(6.59)	(0.29)	(0.22)	(1.63)	
	N	52,505,504	52,505,504	52,505,504	52,063,160	52,552,864	

Notes: Each cell of the table is a separate regression. States OH, RI, TN, VA, and WA use the specification in Equation (2), while SC uses the specification in Equation (3). All regressions estimate the discontinuity at the time of the law change, using non-law-change as controls and linear trends before and after the change. Regressions have controls for macroeconomic factors and seasonal factors, and have standard errors clustered at the state level. * denotes significance at the 10% level, ** denotes significance at the 5% level, and *** denotes significance at the 1% level.

TABLE 6. Customer Selection in States with Large Drops in Volume

State	Repeat Borrower in Pre-Period?	Probability of Appearance in Post-Period	Odds Ratio Yes/No
SC	No	16.2%	4.34
	Yes	45.6%	
Other States	No	17.2%	5.28
	Yes	52.3%	
VA	No	18.6%	2.77
	Yes	38.8%	
Other States	No	23.5%	5.61
	Yes	63.3%	
WA	No	11.4%	4.82
	Yes	38.3%	
Other States	No	18.0%	5.37
	Yes	54.1%	

Notes: Repeat Borrower defined as any borrower whose pre-period loans led to indebtedness 3 months after origination a greater proportion of the time than was the median for all pre-period borrowers. A borrower is considered to appear in the post-period if he or she takes any loan in the post-period. Pre- and post-periods defined by state, with SC using its second law change. Odds ratios calculated as $\frac{p_1}{1-p_1} / \frac{p_2}{1-p_2}$.

www.ingramcontent.com/pod-product-compliance
Lightning Source LLC
Chambersburg PA
CBHW081805170526
45167CB00008B/3336